THE BLACK MAN'S GUIDE TO ROMANCING THE BLACK WOMAN

Things Every Man Should
Know About Every Woman

Dale J. Kelly

FOREWORD BY PHILLIP G. CARGILE

authorHOUSE™

1663 LIBERTY DRIVE, SUITE 200
BLOOMINGTON, INDIANA 47403
(800) 839-8640
WWW.AUTHORHOUSE.COM

First published by AuthorHouse 07/19/05

ISBN: 1-4208-6243-X (sc)

Library of Congress Control Number: 2005904992

Printed in the United States of America
Bloomington, Indiana

This book is printed on acid-free paper.

TABLE OF CONTENTS

DEDICATION

This book is dedicated to the one woman whom I have romanced since January 1, 1997. You are my best friend, my love, my wife, and my life. You're the reason why I breathe, my inspiration, and without you I would be just a shell of a man.

With Gratitude

Thanks to my children for putting up with me during the completing of this book. Christopher, learn how to treat women from this and Carina learn how to be treated by a man from this. This is your legacy, your roadmap from Dad, use it wisely and you too will be as happy with someone as I am with your mother.

Special Thanks To

Phillip Cargile, my writing mentor, thanks for inspiring me to return to school and continuing my education. Had it not been for your book, *"Old Friends and Married People"*, this book or my degree would not have come to fruition. God has blessed you with a wonderful wife and family; continue acknowledging him in all your ways. See you on the tour!

Major John Sayre whose insight and good advice gave me the motivation to finish this book. Southern Ohio College lost a great professor but I gained a good friend.

Lela L. King and Everett A. Cork of **Second Chance Productions, Inc.,** for always believing in my gift of writing. You took a chance on me and it paid off. You are my heroes and pen pals for life. Mary Nagel and Chase Anderson of **KAN Productions** wait until we produce the movie version. This is only the beginning.

Minister A. Robbin Boozer for your assistance with "Church Women vs. Christian Women". God bless you and Sydney on your romantic journey to happiness. Who would have thought we'd both find our spouses in Illinois?

Pastor Kazavah (KZ) Smith, his beautiful wife Connie, and the Corinthian Baptist Church family for all you support over the years. You have been a special part of my life since 1996 and I love you all.

The Southern Ohio College Crew

Ayita, Keasha, George, Travis, Jeff Cooper, Glen Rutherford, H. Michelle Toney, Ms. Carol, Doug Yeager (the Chairman), Jeff Winkleman, Bill Simmons, Dennis Garza-Mapps, the ladies in the front office, Vickie, Brandy and the rest of you "...Dale's here"!

Dialysis Specialist of Fairfield

Keri O., Angel, Jonathon, Carol, Ramona, Christopher, Todd, Vickie, Terri, Jody, Danielle and everyone else past and present, thank you. I will not forget your contribution to this book during my early morning research.

FOREWORD

Okay now you've got it, and the next step is to read it. Reading is the ultimate form of one-way communication straight to the brain. And this is just where this novel will take you. "The Black Man's Guide to Romancing the Black Woman," is not a mind tease but a curiosity pleaser with insights on how you can dance your way into a Black woman's heart. Too often Black women have been viewed as an achievement or an acquired taste for those that wanted to say they've dated out of their race. Worst of all the Black man often have misunderstood the Nubian Princess as being too much trouble; too hard to understand and get along with compared to women of a different ethnic backgrounds. In this multi-cultural society we live in, it's good to read a novel that identifies Black women as a complicated but beautiful creation of God. Whether you are in a relationship or considering being in one this will be a good read that will add value to your individual style of communication. So go on, read it, enjoy it, then read it again and be educated by it.

Phillip G. Cargile
Gp Books

About The Author

Dale J. Kelly is married to Nina Kelly (nee Weems) and resides in Fairfield, Ohio with two of their four children, Christopher 12 and Carina 11. They each have adult children, Peyton (Nina) and Mercedes (Dale), and between them eight grandchildren. Dale was born and raised in neighboring Cincinnati, Ohio where he graduated from Western Hills High in 1979. After graduation he attended Wilberforce University and later transferred to Betz College for Business.

Dale has spent the past 30-years in Communication and Entertainment, seventeen of those years as radio announcer on several local Cincinnati stations (including the second oldest black owned station in the country AM 1480 WCIN) playing gospel, Classic Soul, Top 40, and the Blues. He is also a gospel singer, songwriter, recording artist, producer, and music publisher. He is the Creative Director of Second Chance Productions Incorporated, a small Black theatrical production company and a noted playwright with several plays to his credit. Dale is also an award winning video producer and Creative Director of KAN Productions. In the fall of 2002, he enrolled in AEC Southern Ohio College where he received an AAS degree in Audio Video Production in June 2004.

In 1996, Dale suffered an anorectic attack that later turned into a major surgery in February 1997. It was during this time that he felt God had a real purpose for his life and while he was recuperating he sought to find what it was. In September 2000, he was diagnosed with End Stage Renal Failure and began dialysis immediately. Despite the physical set backs he decided to continue and further his education. Although familiar with the charge of writing songs, short stories, and plays he took an interest in this writing challenge. "It began as another play hopeful but I continued to write and it took on the life of a book because I had so much to say".

Considered permanently disabled, due to kidney failure, Dale has not lost his focused and is already working on his next book; the sequel to this first book, "Lyrical Romance", a book of romantic stories and poetry. "My illness may have changed my lifestyle but my family still has to survive. I never understood the meaning of quit and I don't plan to ever do it. My sole motivation is making sure God gets out of me everything he put in me to reach anyone who is facing life as I have. Never give up, never give in, and never give out."

"This book is also dedicated to the memory of my sons Michael Edward and Isaiah Kelly. Four of the best friends I've known, Keith Oliver who taught me how to be a DJ, eat pizza with black olives and make the best pitcher of kool-aid. Anthony Jackson who saw something in me when I couldn't see it for myself. Edward B. Brown (Eddie B.) whose voice and friendship is missed more than you'll ever know and Vickie Lee, one of God's greatest gifts to the world. Finally to my grandfather Elmer Roy Taylor (Poppa) and first cousin Christopher L. Taylor (it's not the same without you man) I miss you all …but I will see you again".

To my spiritual brother Lionel (L. B.) Bassett Sr., God is calling for you to keep standing in everything you do. When you done all to stand, keep standing. Our time is now because the Lord has made it so.

CHAPTER I

THE FIRST STEP

The first black woman I fell in love with was my grandmother. I was just a boy but I quickly learned that this woman loved me for whom and what I was. Although I did not have much to offer her, she taught me how to love in spite of all the other life lessons I would soon learn as I grew into my manhood. As I was growing up, my mother was very influential in my life but with much conflict. I saw her as a strong black woman who didn't take any mess from anyone. After becoming an adult, I later found out that she wasn't as strong as she could have been. Despite her weaknesses, she taught me how to take care of my household. She challenged my male ego and questioned my views about women by asking me what kind of husband I thought I would be to my wife. When I look back my mother is the woman who was the architect to building my character as a black man. Now, I'm no expert on women or even romancing them, but, I know what I know from experience and if my experience helps you then you're reading the right book. I'm no Dr. Phil, but he hasn't had the life I've had and yet somehow I think he would agree with me.

What is romance? Well, I'm not going to keep you in suspense; it's not a night out at dinner, dancing, the theater, or a movie. It's not a picnic lunch or a date at the museum. It's not the club scene and definitely not booty call. These are just *love games*. I'm a major fan of romantic stories because they have always intrigued me what the boy does to get the girl then lose the girl only to get the girl back. Or what the girl does to attract the boy then, use the boy only to realize she's in love with him. Most people think that like chivalry, romance is dead. "Romance is about the possibility in a thing. It's about the first time a man asks a woman out until the first time he makes love to her or when a man asks a woman to marry him until the time she says I do. When a couple who's been together for a long period of time says there's no more romance, what they're really saying is they've exhausted the possibilities." **(Darius Lovehall; Love Jones, 1997)** There is no <u>real</u> definitive description of romance because it is a learned behavior. We absorb what we see from our parents, grandparents, neighbors, where we go to church, or the club. It's the portrayal that we perceive from music videos, the movies, and even romantic novels. We take a little bit from each and try to emulate or incorporate these different styles into our own romantic activities.

I believe romance keeps a person on his toes and fully alive because it has an element of surprise from day to day. A card, a phone call, or even a five-minute visit will warm the heart and keep the romance energetic because it keeps the possibility and hope in a relationship. Romance is expressed in many ways but one has to be true to one's self. Whatever you do fellows, be consistent, let her see you **for who you really are** and not someone you're trying to be. What happens as a result of this? You get together and she tries to change you back to your false self. When the *"real you"* comes out it ends with a break up and with each relationship this pattern is repeated. Make sure she's the one you truly want to romance, but don't use romance as a game because it will hurt you in the end.

You will not find romance or anything like it on talk shows such as Ricki Lake, Jerry Springer or shows like them. These types of shows exploit black people all for the sake of "five minutes of fame" (of course, this is one man's opinion) and continue the very myth that black men, in particular, are not inherently romantic. These shows continue to exploit the players, so-called pimps, thugs, gangstas, and wanna-bes whose only goal in life is to see how many babies' mommas they can accumulate or how many "hoes" they can hit. "The misogyny articulated by the hip hop generation comes from its marginalization by a welfare system that defines "family" as a woman with children and a check from AFDC or child support. It's not just the demise of work in urban American that has alienated Black men from the family-supporting and child rearing positions they used to occupy with pride; it's a welfare/child support system that has substituted for them. Its 30-years of Black male dislocation that's moved us from the R & B of 25 years ago – "Ain't No Woman Like The One I've Got" – to such lyrics as "Bitches Ain't Nuthin But Hoes and Tricks."[1]

This very attitude comes from the slave master's mentality while owning blacks and using them as breeders. Black male slaves were forced to have sex with black female slaves in order to populate the master's plantations and then sold like horses, which caused much of the permanent separation of the black family. So the "*bred to breed*" attitude has been perpetuated through Black American history and thus black men in this country have not traditionally been romantic and black women have just accepted the status quo. Black fathers, as an unwritten rule, have not taught their sons how to romance black woman and so the cycle of mistreating our counterparts continues and black women have a hard time choosing the right man. "About 8 percent of American households can be categorized as female-headed households with children, but there is significant variation in the share of female-headed households by race and ethnicity. In 2002, about 5 percent of non-Hispanic white and Asian households were headed by women with children. In contrast, single mothers with kids accounted for 22 percent of all black households. Over the past 25 years, the percentage of female-headed households with children has increased particularly rapidly among blacks, but this trend appears to have slowed during the last five years."[2]

Where does the romance begin? Let's say for the sake of argument that romance begins with an attraction. Boy sees girl, girl sees boy, he is attracted to girl but girl is not to him, why? Because the attraction was not mutual, it was simply physical. He wasn't what the girl was looking for and consequently his advances turned her off. Likewise, girl is attracted to boy but boy is not to girl because she is not what he wants and so he is also turned off. Attraction has to be mutual, not necessarily physical. Thus the differences between lust and romance are mental and physical. Can you guess which is which? In other words, there has to be a mental agreement between both parties before the attraction goes any further. It has to be more than just a physical thing (lust) to being attracted to someone. This is what I refer to as the "call and respond" method; is there dialogue, is it intellectual, and is it stimulating? Is there eye contact, is there mutual flirting, can you spiritually feel one another, and is there humor? Is he funny, does she make you laugh, are you both laughing at the same things, and what was the joke?

When you think about the relationships you've been involved in, do you remember how they started? Can you remember what attracted you to her or him? Fellows, you have to consider that most of the women you meet have been in relationships prior to you. So when you come along, you have the awesome task of proving that you're not the other guy. Assuming she's never been romanced before and you're the first, then you have some work to do. It's not fair, I know, but that's how it is especially when you're dealing with a seasoned "sista" who is much more experienced with affairs of the heart than some of these younger women. No disrespect to you younger sisters but because of your inexperience how is it remotely possible that you know what to look for in a man, when basically all you do is club hop. Remember, where you meet a man is all apart of his on-going lifestyle. It's reasonable to say history has proven that mothers have not taught their daughters how to be romanced because they weren't romanced. And so you learn by trial and error.

Several questions come to mind when thinking about romance. Who are the examples of romance for the black community? Who gives us genuine steps to follow when we are pursuing our journey of romance? Who sets the guidelines for romance? When we see past images of romantic figures, black women usually refer to Bill Dee Williams and black men refer to Pam Grier. These however in truth were just sexy images. But today's images are more in numbers and just as attractive as the images of the past. *Morris Chestnut, Taye Diggs, Blair Underwood, Ice Cube, Gabrielle Union, Halle Berry, Queen Latifah, and Nia Long* just to name a few. They portray images of romance in some of their movies that we actually pay to see. Brown Sugar, Poetic Justice, Jason's Lyric, and The Best Man to name a few. Herein lies the lesson, if you're going to pay to see them, take notes and get your moneys worth. Believe me; if art imitates life then likewise life should imitate art, especially when it comes to romance.

When we talk about the "seasoned sista" we're describing a more mature woman from about the age of 40 and up. These women have been there done that more times than they care to count but their experience is invaluable. They have a much better idea of what kind of man they will deal with and usually will not except anything less. The reason for this is most of them have everything tangible you could offer: their own home, car, and money. They can take care of themselves better than you and if children are involved; they're mostly grown and on their own. So the only thing left is romance, and how do you accomplish that? From all the women I've interviewed, they tell me "you have come correct." Most women are not looking for "a boy" they're looking for "a man." This is the first step to romance; **YOU HAVE TO BE A MAN**. One who is responsible for himself, his actions, takes care of business, and handles things in a mature way. Most importantly, you have to first respect and love yourself.

There is no magical formula to romancing the black woman- it's just a learning experience. Just as we grow from being toddlers to little boys to young men to adult men, we learn more about ourselves, our desires, and what kind of woman we'd like in our lives. The first model of that woman usually is our mothers or grandmothers. Growing up I remember going to my grandmother's home every weekend to see her. I just couldn't get enough of her hugging me and kissing me on my forehead. I felt safe in her arms but mostly I felt loved. She would remind me of the times when I was a toddler how we went for walks in the neighborhood and then she'd take me home for a nap. I didn't know then that the woman I would later fall in love with would have some of the same attributes as my grandmother- the first woman who poured love into me. The amount of love they (black women) pour into us determines how we treat woman …and you know this. Women look for signs like how respectful you are to your mother or what kind of relationship you have with her. Believe me, this is a major factor when deciding whether or not to have any kind of on-going relationship with you. So as you read this book remember it is a guide to romancing the black woman, a journey to a place you've probably never been before.

An old wives tale is to see how a man treats his mother, children, and pets. Children and pets are often better judges of character than adults. They feel and don't rationalize like adults do.

"The vision of Lyndon B. Johnson's "Great Society" (1966) started on poverty, "but in hindsight America made a war on Black fathers, i.e., male head of households, inasmuch as the ill-conceived social programs became a Trojan horse that turned African-American families upside down. Whether it was America's intent, or not most federal programs devalued Black fathers.

History records those Black males; whose job description is "laborer" was put in a tenuous position of being unable to pay the cost to be the boss in their own homes. It's difficult for a Black man to head a household, when even his kids can generate more income from social programs than he does working on menial, low paying jobs. That sad fact was exacerbated when Black females became a double minority, ergo, affirmative action opened doors for less threatening Black women, instead of their men. Lest we forget, many social programs favored welfare mothers, who had no man in the house. Denial notwithstanding, independent, economically empowered Black female's rap was just as demeaning to Black males that have been excluded by LBJ's Great Society vision.

Many black male's spirits were grievously wounded, after their meager finances negated romances and they became more of a liability than an asset for their families. The welfare system, indeed, allows single mothers to live better on government assistance than on poor husband's salary. Henceforth, while it wasn't put into music, or backed up by a beat, "you ain't helping, you can get to stepping, because I can do bad by myself," it's definitely a popular rap, that top's the list on Black America's dysfunctional family charts."[3]

━━━━━►•◄━━━━━

CHAPTER II

TAKE YOUR TIME

There are three things black men need to know about taking their time. First, you need to slow down and not move so fast because women do not like to be rushed into a relationship. Second, you need to understand that women do not want to be rushed into sex. Third, you need to realize that most women are not in a hurry to meet your mother, because this could mean potential commitment and you just started dating. Each of these will come in time but you must wait until she is ready.

You need to "woo" her, "court" her or just "date" her, but don't start something you cannot continue. Janet Jackson sings a song entitled, "Let's wait a While" before we go too far. In this song she explains to her man that it's important not to rush into sex, let's not do something we'll regret. Likewise, Al Green sings, "Let's Stay Together" where he explains to his woman that he's willing to do whatever she wants to do because of how she makes him feel. Remember romance is about the possibilities in a relationship. So from the first time you ask her out until such time the two of you decide to take things farther, make each moment together a memorable one.

I always say "if you put it out there, then do something with it"; you have to show you care until you stop caring. This doesn't mean you have to spend a great deal of money, it just means how you get her is how you'll keep her. You must make her feel like she's important to you which means you'll have to take the time to really get to know her. When I was dating I made it an important factor to get to know my companion in order to make the date a smooth one. Remember, you are dealing with a black queen and she expects you to act as a black king. It's the little things that matter to most women, for instance, after a period of time has passed in your relationship while she's in the shower write a love note on the steamed mirror. After she's had a hard day at work invite her to your place using love notes to direct her every move until she is greeted with a hot scented bubble bath and afterwards a full body massage with scented body oils. Maybe one day when she least expects it, send a bouquet of flowers or roses with a note from you stating, "Just thinking about you." Little things lead to countless possibilities.

Flirting is an excellent way to begin a relationship because if she is receptive to your advances then you may have a chance. Flirting is also a great way to keep the romance exciting, but it doesn't have to be overwhelming. In the beginning try not to come on too strongly with her because you could scare her away. For example, not every woman goes for a "thug-like" man with a mouth full of gold or platinum somehow this just defeats the purpose. However, a man who is articulate and has a sense of humor is a definite winner. Also, be careful of the woman who finds flirting as challenging as you do, her only interest is to test your masculinity. When I was in my mid 20's, I met a woman who was 40. I was with friends at a quaint little restaurant in Dayton, Ohio when she came over to our table. After being introduced to her I began to flirt as I had done so many other times before. She began to flirt back and caught me off guard …and I choked. This was the one time I was totally out of my league; she thought it was cute, but I was embarrassed. I wasn't prepared for this and could not respond quickly enough to her advances. She really put my skills to the test and I blew it. Fellows make sure you are on top of your game and that your flirting skills are strong enough to "back it up".

No two persons ever flirt the same way -everyone has their own style; and there are some who don't flirt at all. While many of you may not know how to flirt I encourage you to learn. Men, I know some of you are shy and afraid to approach most women but its okay …they won't bite unless you ask them! Flirting is another way of easing the tension like having a good sense of humor. But if you're not good at it then go for what you know. Some years ago a friend of mine told me a story about two bulls sitting on top of a hill. They were looking down at the cows at the foot of the hill. The younger bull was jumping up and down saying to the older bull, "come on let's run down there and get us one of them". The older bull looked at the young bull and then the cows at the foot of the hill and replied, "Son you run down there and get you one, I'm going to walk and get them all".

It is very important for the "seasoned brothers" to take the younger brothers under their wings, sit them down, and get them straight. But you older brothers are usually set in your ways and don't want to be bothered. My father didn't do this with me but I am passing these skills on to my son because it's a lonely world out there without a good woman to share it with. The Godfather of Soul recorded "It's a man's world but it would be nothing without a woman or a girl". [4]

Some of you think that just because you're in a committed relationship, your flirting days are over. Think again. After all, flirting is just making her feel good about herself and you feeling even better because you've made your partner feel good. Try to get back in the mindset when you first met her. Go back to giving compliments generously and sincerely, but also use body language. Lean close when you're talking. Wink at her from across the room no matter where you are. Hold hands while walking down the street or in the park. When you're home alone just spontaneously grab her and begin to slow dance in the middle of the room. Before you know it you'll be flirting all the time.

Women enjoy articulate men who are not afraid to openly share about themselves or their feelings. It's okay to ask questions but don't get so personal too quickly, let her tell you about herself, her life experiences, and her feelings. Be a good listener. Feel free to ask what she likes and dislikes in order not to make the mistake of upsetting her because you did something she didn't like. Never compare her to another woman this is a no-no. It's okay that she knows you're a single parent; this is attractive in some cases. Hopefully she will see a more responsible you and not the "baby's momma drama" you may have to contend with. Don't be a deadbeat dad and she finds out about it, your romancing days are over! Plus, don't ever impose your children on her even if you're looking for a new mommy, she may just leave you looking. Remember we're talking about romancing the Black Woman, finding a partner for yourself, not finding a babysitter for your children.

CHAPTER III

JEALOUSY

One of the issues facing some couples is the "green-eyed monster" known as jealousy. It has caused more problems and break-ups even before the romance has had a chance to blossom. The romantic journey has to face some adversities, but there is no room for jealousy it'll disturb the flow of things. So what? She's beautiful; don't let your pride get in the way of a good thing. So what if other men look at her, this just means they're envious of what you have ...but she's with you ...and she loves you. Remember, some women enjoy attention but it doesn't have to be so overwhelming that it begins to smother her. If you expect to keep her attention then save the drama for your ...and you know this!

This should be the number one rule in the handbook for men. Don't ever compare her to another woman, because women don't like that; not your ex-girlfriend, ex-wife, and specifically not your mother especially if you're a momma's boy ...keep that to yourself. Put yourself in a woman's place at the grocery checkout. How many magazines are there "in your face" fostering jealousies and comparison of women? A zillion. Men really need to understand that through advertising, women get bombarded daily with the message that they aren't "adequate enough" as they are. So why put salt in their wounds by comparing them to someone else in your life? It's so hurtful. And when a woman is in pain, there isn't much room for romance.

There are some women with low self-esteem and are not very secure with themselves. So they're jealous of the attraction you may receive from other women. It is imperative for you to assure and reassure her that you're focused on her. Now let's not be ignorant, it is a fact that men look at women and women look at men this is how the attraction begins. However, looking is not the same as touching. Touching creates more problems than you need, this is the lesson you learn when you are romancing a woman who has been burnt a few times. This is why it is so necessary for black men to be honest and up front with black women because they are like delicate flowers that have been picked on already and need to be handled with care. You have to be supportive, nurturing, and learn how to give her some space in order for her to keep her own individuality.

Confidence is a very attractive quality to most women but arrogance will get you nowhere. Be positive and try to keep all negative influences out of a potential relationship. Your confidence may rub off on her if she is in need of it. Remember, you have to be secure in yourself and grounded because things like jealousy are just a sign of weakness and insecurity. Strong black women intimidate some black men but that's only because of their own insecurities. A black woman who is strong has need of a strong black man that respects her, and she knows to always let him be a man because she's a woman.

Food for thought: what is good about jealousy? Is it a warning or a sign that your partner feels ignored? Are men or women more jealous? This can lead to an abusive relationship.

Jealousy: At the beginning of a relationship an abuser will always say that jealousy is a sign of love; jealousy has nothing to do with love, it's a sign of possessiveness and lack of trust. It's also a sign of major insecurities that one person has of himself or herself. The abuser will question the woman about whom she talks to, accuse her of flirting, or be jealous of time she spends with family, friends, or children. As jealousy progresses, the abuser may call her frequently or drop by unexpectedly. The abuser may refuse to let her work for fear she will meet someone else, or even do strange things such as checking her car mileage or asking friends to watch her. If this is you or someone you know, get help now!

Baggage: This is one of those things that some people bring to a relationship that causes too many problems. If you're in relationship where you have some baggage from a past relationship then you need to take a break from this woman. Why? Because she's never going to measure up to the last thing you had in your life. Furthermore, you cannot expect nor should you expect this present relationship to help you get over the past. That's unfair! If you haven't gotten over it by now …get some therapy. I was discussing this topic with a new friend at dinner and he told me how bad his first marriage was and how it ended. Let me preface his story. He's a really nice guy, hard worker, in his 40's, single, great cook, loves old school, respects older people, and is a good father.

We were talking about a play I had written and produced entitled "Pen Pals", where Lenora is explaining to Quincy in a letter why she relocated to his city to live. She had been married for twenty years to the same man and on the day they were to celebrate their 20th wedding anniversary, she comes home to find him in bed not only with another woman but her best friend from childhood. She was devastated and all he (her husband) could say was "it's not what it looks like baby", she replied "with her feet pointed to the ceiling and yours pointed straight to hell, what else would it look like?" So she left him and lost her best friend in the process. This is baggage she could have carried for the remainder of her life but she understood that in order to move forward she had to get over her past and progress on with her life. So she spends the next full year being Quincy's pen pal getting to know one another on many levels until they decided to finally meet only to find out that they been living across the hall from each other and never spoke a single word.

Unfortunately, this similar thing happened to my new friend. He came home only to find his wife in bed with another man. He too was devastated by the mere audacity of her attitude; it was as though she didn't care. Needless to say he divorced her with prejudice and later found himself in another relationship where this female companion was sleeping with her first cousin. Imagine his shock! He quickly left her, relocated to another city, and for 2 ½ years he hasn't been involved with another woman because he's so afraid of something happening again. He simply has too much baggage, and quite honestly he doesn't need to be involved in a relationship until he has completely gotten over his past. Here's what will happen, he'll have too many trust issues. He'll substitute his feelings for her with loving her family because his family is not with him. He'll also bend over backwards to make her happy at the expense of his own happiness because he doesn't want to be lonely. But he will not intentionally mistreat her and they will forever be friends; and who knows she may be the one.

Just as Quincy and Lenora learned about each other on many levels, he too needs to invest the same kind of uncomplicated effort in some black queen who is willing to make him her king. No jealousy, no baggage, no stress.

CHAPTER IV

FINANCIALLY CREATIVE

When you decide to take a woman out you should only pay for what you can afford but don't be cheap …be creative. If you're not Michael Jordan, then don't try to spend like him. Your first dinner out should cost no more than $50 dollars. If a theater or a movie is included, then spend no more than $90 dollars and don't expect sex after the date. Now, there are those who can spend like M. J. but you'll have to be very careful of the infamous "gold diggers". They're everywhere you go and looking to get as deep into your pockets as you will let them and willing to pay the price. You don't have to buy her a dress because believe it or not she's got a closet full of clothes. Don't allow her to make you think you have to get her "hair did" or "nails did" believe me she's got the money to take care of that herself. Don't be frugal, be smart; use wisdom. *Don't ever feel like you have to pay for a woman's time, unless you're into that sort of thing, because your time is just as valuable as hers. More importantly, women should not ever feel like she has a dollar price on her because this makes her weak and vulnerable. Her strength is in her independence and not depending on a man to validate her as a woman.*

You've acquired talents over the years …use them! You need to have a great sense of humor and use what ever you excel at to make your romancing journey more fun than you could've imagined. One of the best things you could do is cook. My very first date with Nina (although she swears it was our second); I prepared a five-course dinner. It began with fresh strawberries dip in honey and chilled, shrimp cocktails with White Zinfandel, a garden salad with two types of dressings, broiled chicken breast over linguini with home-made Alfredo sauce and kool-aid (every home should have kool-aid). For dessert I made a Strawberry cheesecake and served it with more White Zinfandel. We left from my place and went to an old school concert only to return back to my place for a nightcap. I figured this dinner date would have cost me exactly $95 dollars not including gas for the car, but since I prepared the dinner myself I saved about $65 dollars. My point is that you have to let her see you perform in the arena that allows you to be yourself.

Before I met Nina, I dated a few times. I remember going out with this wonderful black woman. We had much in common and did quite a bit together. I took her out to eat for lunch once and didn't realize I couldn't cover the check for the two of us. I pretended to go to the restroom and went to the nearest ATM only to find that I had enough money to feed her and have a soda for myself. This was embarrassing but I got through it all right. I tried too hard to impress her and it backfired. She could have been indignant about it but she was very understanding and we laughed about it because I had to be honest and tell her what I had done. She still ate her meal and I had free refills on my soda. There is a twofold lesson here, (1) always be honest and check your finances before you take a woman out and (2) never let her see you sweat.

Don't be intimidated by other men who may be more attractive than you remember, she's with you. There are things you can do to make the romancing experience more interesting by the minute. For instance, rent 6 movies, two comedies, two dramas, and two romances. Microwave some popcorn and chill a bottle of your favorite non-alcoholic beverage or cook a small pot of chili and chill a bottle of your favorite wine. Spend a Friday or Saturday evening cuddled up on a pallet watching the movies or playing a romantic game of Q. & A. Turn on some Isley Brothers or Teddy P. or Musiq Soul Child and get your slow dance on.

The focal point of romance is to create memorable moments that last a lifetime. Sure you'll have those moments when you have a fight (argument) with one another but at the end of the day when all has been said and done, what keeps you together? Are there enough memorable moments that have solidified your relationship? Are you remembering the small things that keep the fires burning? Are you still laughing together and what was the joke?

An imagination is free …the results priceless.

There is no real definitive description of romance because it is a learned behavior. We absorb what we see… and incorporate these different styles into our own romantic activities.

Being financially creative doesn't mean that you have to buy dozens of roses when one single rose will do. This is just another way of throwing money at her to impress her when all she's really looking for is a sincere heart. Maybe you handpicked a daisy from somebody's garden without getting caught; it's sweeter than a bouquet of carnations. Get a fish bowl or an old cookie jar and fill it with love fortunes. (And you thought fortunes only came in cookies!) Use small colorful pieces of paper and write various things you love about her. Tell her how beautiful her brown eyes are, or how her smile lights up an entire room, or how it's so hard to breath without her. All these show that you took the time and made the effort to say how much you care.

Chapter V

———➤•0•◀———

Sincererity

Women enjoy men who are not phony and do not put on airs. If you start right then you'll ultimately end right, with a relationship. Women have this keen sense of detecting liars, so the best way to deal with them is to be up front. You are not obligated to tell her your life story but you can tell her what you want her to know without deceiving her. There are some things about you that may be interesting to her but don't overwhelm her by being braggadocios. One of my "warning signs" in black men is; **if *you are totally in love with yourself, then how much room in your heart do you have for a partner, or for romance for that matter?*** When you're into the relationship don't be afraid to express to her things like her breath is fowl or her hair needs to be done or even the scent she is wearing doesn't smell right. Don't be harsh; say it in a loving way because she'll respect the fact that you cared enough to say something. Trust me, if it were you, she'd tell you! You also have to compliment her every chance you get because if she wasn't so beautiful to you, you wouldn't have taken the time to go after her.

Women notice everything about men from the shoes to his head. Shoes, socks (what color and are they mix-matched?), pants, shirt, shirt-collar, hands, fingernails, facial hair, teeth, breath, height, and any distinguishing marks. So men should pay just as much attention to women. Try to make it your business to know her favorite perfume, her favorite type of dress clothes, how she looks in pumps (high heels), and can she walk in them. What is her favorite drink? Is her breath minty or sweet smelling? Is that her hair or is her weave out of place? Concentrate on her and no other woman so she may feel special, like she's the center of your attention. I know this sounds like "ego stroking", but she'd do the same for you because she wants her man to look right at all times …even in a pair of jeans. Here's the lesson, if you make sure your queen is treated royally, then your queen will give you the royal treatment of a king.

Romance is to sensuality as lust is to sexuality. Although they may seem similar there are differences. Lust is an uncontrolled physical condition while romance is a controlled mental emotion. Sometimes we allow lust to get the better of us because of a sexual orgasm. Romance does the same, only mental, and leaves us desiring for more. The ultimate goal is to achieve both at the same time …talk about a mind-blowing experience. Every relationship is different; of course we all understand that, but there are countless possibilities. Contrary to popular belief women are not from Venus and men are not from Mars but we are very different. We do however; share some of the same emotions we just present them differently. When I was growing up during the 60's & 70's, you could always tell when a brother was feeling down about his love life by the music he played. Back then, the music spoke for us, it transcended our feelings, and it made everything seem all right. It was the Dells singing "Stay in My Corner", or Marvin Gaye singing "If This World Were Mine", or The Isley Brothers singing "For the Love of You".

Whatever it was you knew what this man was saying to his woman and you knew he was sincere.

It's about sincerity not about how smooth you are or how strong your rap is or even how much "game you can spit", its how you approach her –from the heart. Brothers, set aside your pride, your strong blackness, and your super-egos for just a moment. Let's be men about this thing. The black queen is so important to our race and America is indebted to her for being the backbone of our country not to mention she is the first lady of the world. If in fact we agree, then according to some of you brothers out there, she should be revered as a queen. Adorned with majesty, gold, diamonds, and the finest of scents …right? Then why not romance her; doesn't she deserve that much from us? Why do we continue to mistreat, disrespect, and hurt the very part of us that gave us life? It's from the heart that we should recognize gratitude for her and acknowledge how vital she is to us. We owe her our thanks and appreciation for her continuous love. We have gained our strength from her whether we want to admit or not, so we owe her our strength in return. You ought to be real when you approach the black woman and come from within when romancing her.

Romance is not a relationship but the possibility in it. Romance includes several attributes that are required to maintain a healthy and vibrant relationship. Patience, tolerance, understanding, communication, and humility are all things that you will encounter during this relationship. They are not to weaken you but instead make you a stronger person. Black women have endured so much from black men that they've made up their minds who they will and will not be involved with. They know who and what they need in their lives. So don't attempt to play the "daddy role" because I'm sure she has or had a father. Don't try to psychoanalyze her because you're probably not qualified; she has friends for that. Don't try to make her happy! WHAT? Well, you have to understand we can't make women happy, that should already be built in them. Every person is responsible for his or her own happiness, but trying to please her is acceptable. You have to know the difference.

Many black women prefer black men who are sincere and good hearted, not control freaks. This is one of those issues that some black men have. It's okay to take control of a situation that needs some order to it, but to try and control her is totally out of the question. Whoever told you that a woman needs to be controlled, simply lied. That's like saying that blacks in America need to be controlled by whites even though slavery was abolished several hundred years ago. Here's a warning sign to black women everywhere; if your man is a control freak and you feel uncomfortable with him or maybe fearful of him …get out now! This is not the right man for you. Don't let your low self-esteem get the best of you, buck-up and get to steppin'. This is not a sincere man this is a man with sincere issues.

Saying "thank you" is one of the most under-utilized phrases in the love-relationship lexicon. After you've been with her for a while, you sometimes take her for granted. A certain amount of granted-taking is acceptable, but that doesn't mean you should forget the niceties. Don't just thank her for giving you the last glass of kool-aid—thank her for saying, "yes" to your first date. Don't just tell her how much you appreciate her for being there for you when you lost your job, or got sick, or for cheering you up through good and bad times, show her how much you appreciate her. And remember, appreciation begets appreciation.

➤◆◄

Chapter VI

Self-esteem

An older black woman taught me that experience is the best teacher. I learned this lesson the hard way by trial and error. *When it comes to affairs of the heart don't fall for the first thing that smiles at you …most black women don't. You have to learn how to guard your heart and use wisdom because some people are like chameleons; they're inconsistent. They change emotional colors from person to person.*

During my freshman year at Wilberforce University (1979 – 1980) I had some self-esteem issues. My level of confidence was at an all time low when it came to women. I was enrolled in a Public Speaking class. I chose a topic that caused me to face my fears up close and personal. The topic was "Love, Romance, & Relationships on a Black College Campus. I interviewed more than a hundred females between the ages of 18 and 25, all students and all involved at one time or another with a black male. As I listened to each young woman express her feelings and emotions about the subject, I began to understand what most men were missing in a relationship, we don't listen. We're too busy trying to be players that we end up hurting some really great women. As I grew into manhood

I learned the art of flirting and how to make a woman feel like a person not just an object. I no longer have self-esteem issues.

We all have some self-esteem issues about one thing or another but it doesn't have to ruin our lives. Brothers, you have to stop going to the party and standing against the wall …ask the lady to dance! It's not like you're trying to marry her just dance with her. **BLACK WOMEN, WOULD YOU PLEASE STOP SHOOTING BROTHERS DOWN AT THE PARTY!** Just speaking from experience brothers, when you're on the dance floor other women are watching to see how you move and deciding whether or not they will dance with you. One of my favorite rap artist is Ludacris and he performs this song entitled, "When I Move You Move," which to me says it all. Fellows learn from watching a woman on the dance floor to see how she moves, this helps you decide if you're in her league or not. Women are always watching men, other women, but mostly the competition.

I have this friend who is drop dead gorgeous in her 40's and involved with a man who could care less about her. The sad part is that her self-esteem is really low because she feels like she can't do without a man. She owns her own home, drives a great car, has excellent credit and even adopted a little boy. She has it going on. But this man has lied to her, deceived her, cheated on her, stolen from her and uses emotional blackmail to keep her under his control. This is a woman who could have anyone she wants and as her friend, I can't say anything to her. She has to get through this on her own; and it just breaks my heart. Herein lies the lessons; if it looks like a snake …you know the rest. How a person feels about one's self is transmitted to other people in subtle ways and tells them how you expect to be treated. People with high self-esteem like and respect themselves and expect others to do the same. Lack of self-respect and low self-esteem invites others to treat you accordingly.

Black women who have self-esteem issues need to talk it out with stronger black women who don't have these issues. The Bible says they that are strong must bear the infirmities of the weak; where are you at strong black sisters?

It has been said "we betray ourselves by the lovers we choose." Our choice of mates is directly influenced by our self-esteem: we choose partners who treat us as well or as badly as we think we deserve. The battered woman tolerates an abusive mate because he reflects and reinforces her low opinion of herself. She finds a man who loves her and treats her well to be weak or simply unattractive. The cuckolded husband unconsciously chooses a woman who will be unfaithful because he doesn't believe fidelity is possible. Others will treat us like we treat ourselves or as well as we let them. Even when they start out treating us differently, our pattern of responses soon teaches them what kind of treatment we expect. Showing little reaction to compliments and praise, but strong reaction to criticism, clearly indicates that we're more interested in criticism than praise and encourages others to respond accordingly.

Food for thought: "Appreciating my own worth and importance, having the character to be accountable for myself and to act responsibly toward others".

CHAPTER VII

CHURCH WOMEN VS. CHRISTIAN WOMEN

Christian women who have been through some things are very sincere and understand the "soul of a man". They are willing to do what it takes to be supportive of a Brother. These sisters will stand by their man through good and bad times, sickness and health, until death do they part. They are the genuine "helpmeet" that will not always look like Halle Berry. She has been looked over, messed over, neglected, and taken for granted in other relationships and it has taken you (her Adam) a long time to find her. This means that, as your rib, she may be a little worn down and not up to snuff as she once was. But she shouldn't be overlooked because good things don't always come wrapped in pretty packages; and sometimes she is overlooked because this man has a false idea of what she should look like. He's dreaming of a fantasy woman and not the spiritual woman he really should consider, but only a spiritual man would understand that.[5]

Christian women are firm in their love of Christ, but very insecure with their love for a man because of past abuse. Insecure yes, but never fearful because she realizes that fear is not of God. However, this can go either way for a man or a woman. When I met my wife, Nina, I omitted to tell her a few things about me; not meaning to deceive her but just wanted her to see me for who I was. Our first date I invited her to church and she gladly accepted. We met and had breakfast that morning and then went on to service. When we got there I escorted her to her seat and said I would be back. So she decided to save a seat for me but when she looked up I was entering the pulpit with the other ministers. I believe I also sang that morning which showed her I had a little talent. I didn't tell her I was a minister because I wanted her to get to know the man first. That was the first Sunday in January 1997; we got married the last Sunday of August 1999. It was because of my insecurities that I didn't tell her, not my fear ... and I still romance her today.

In discussing this matter with a good friend of mine, she shared with me that Christian women have been under the Word long enough to know how to be a good wife. They have gone to bible study, Sunday school, and marriage classes because they plan on getting it right, whether it's the first or second time, especially if they've been divorced. Fellows you have to come correct because this sister plans on being the perfect wife according to the Word of God, notwithstanding the work that goes into the marriage.[6] She already knows that the Lord has sent this man to her because she has been fasting and praying for a while. She's waited patiently praying that the Lord will bless her husband, strengthen him, build him up, and hedge him up for years before she even meets him. She's already written their vows because she's committed to him based on the promise of the Lord.[7] All they need to do is sign the certificate.

While the flip side of this coin is the **church woman**, the one who has the weekly ritual of going in the church but the church not going in her. This woman you have to watch because just as Eve was deceived by a snake so is a man deceived by her beauty. This is a sneaky woman that perpetrates Holiness; the Bible calls her a "strange woman".[8] You've heard the saying, "everything that glitters ain't gold," she epitomizes this statement. She doesn't dress for worship she dresses to be worshipped. She's not a bible student but a student of persuasiveness. She doesn't mind sharing a brother as long as she gets what she wants out of him, he can go home to somebody else; thus she doesn't subscribe to the 10 commandments.[9] If he looks good, talks good, and got a little money she'll go after him all in the name of "brotherly love" … yeah right!

Of course there is the churchman that appears, as a wolf in sheep clothing preying on innocent women's feelings and emotions because he hasn't submitted his life totally over to the will of God. He is not a reflection of Godliness but a reflection of ungodliness. He has no spiritual power other than to deceive and destroy the lives of lonely women. His ideal of romance is to wine and dine you, and then have you for dessert. He has the gift of gab and very persuasive with words. He may have a good job and possibly an officer in the church or a church musician (I know quite a few of them that are like this). He's probably been married once or twice and not willing to do it again because he couldn't handle the responsibility of being faithful. So he plays the field. He is not humble like the Christian man whose walk is a walk of faith and reverence for God. Following after Paul's instruction[10] is not in his vocabulary and thus he is really a lonely person.

The Christian woman and man both understand the need to be romanced on a whole other level. Church folk don't get it! Romance is guided by integrity, morality, and spirituality. Church folk are led by flesh. Romance provides a fresh perspective or outlook on a relationship where church folk only see one thing …what's in it for them? Part of the strength of a good black woman comes from her deepened faith in God; the rest comes from her experience with past relationships. Some good and some bad, but all worth it while waiting for the man she's been praying for. The Christian woman has a rebuilt character and desires a man to be a lifelong partner with strong spiritual beliefs, undisturbed faith, and an ongoing personal relationship with his Creator. He has to make God first, family and friends second, and himself third. But she is the most important person in his life because she is, after all, his rib.

CHAPTER VIII

———⊱•◦•⊰———

CHOICES

This chapter is not meant to offend anyone just educate you to the stereotypical way of thinking from our own community. Some black men really look at our black queens and judge them accordingly. <u>Take a deep breath</u> before reading this chapter and don't shoot the messenger.

I was in conversation with a young woman one summer about the attitude of different colored (hues) Black women. She insisted that the lighter of them had more patience than any of the other hues throughout our race. I expressed to her that she had been unequivocally misinformed. For years I've had to deal with the "light skinned black female" beginning with the closest one to me, my sister. She is the lightest of my mother's four children and of course the most impatient. When I was a senior in high school I fathered a daughter by a beautiful light skinned sista'; turns out we went our separate ways after graduation. In college, I met and became overwhelmingly infatuated with a light skinned sista' that could have passed for Caucasian. She didn't feel the same way about me and so we never made a love connection but remained friends. Each of these women had very little patience. There are so many hues of the black woman but not surprisingly each one comes with her own attitude.

The **Light-Skinned** (high yellow) sister is beautiful to look at with her fine hair, well maintained nails, and finely shaped body. She has the ability to capture most black men's attention with just a smile or batting her eyes or even walking away. But she is somewhat precarious in her nature (non-violent of course) and cunning in how she manipulates her prey. Often times she is a part of a "tug-of –war" for her man with another sister of the same complexion. The **Caramel Skinned** (cinnamon) sister is an in between woman who has the ability to be flexible with her looks and her attitude. Some black men find this woman very appealing because she usually has light colored eyes that have commanded his attention and she may or may not be his "show piece." She is usually the one who has his heart more than any other woman he's with.

The **Brown Skinned** (milk chocolate) sister is a desired woman because she is not light and not concerned about her complexion. She has confidence in her looks and usually is not without a man. Her features show a somewhat hidden Indian heritage and she has the body to complete the package. Never count her out of the dating game because if she comes alone to the party, she will not leave alone. Her attitude is smooth until she has to become angry …and believe me, you do not want to get her angry. The **Chocolate Skinned** sister is sometimes confused with the brown skinned sister but she is a little darker. Generally her hair is not as long unless she's wearing a weave, but she has the ability to dress up and enhance her looks. Her dark complexion is as smooth as coco butter, her smile as bright as the stars, and her aroma smells as sweet as honeysuckle in the spring. She is the one woman that some black men stay away from because she is so mysterious. Often times, she is the quite one in a group of women but the one everyone goes to for love advice. The reason for this is because her relationships are not for show and she knows how to please her man without all the outside distraction.

The **Dark Skinned** sister is looked at, as too dark or "I would not be seen with her". The truth of the matter is that some black men prefer her overall the other hues because she is the epitome of the black woman. Her darkness hides all the superficial scars that life causes us each day. On a personal note, this is the woman I married. She is the closest looking to the motherland, Africa, where she resembles the darkest of women. She is strong in her conviction, her faith is unraveled and her family is the most important thing to her.

I've experienced each of these women in my family, and have come to the conclusion that the only differences are the hues. My great-grandmother was one half Indian and Black, her daughter (my grandmother) is dark. My mother is dark, one sister is light and the other sister is brown skinned. My oldest daughter is chocolate and my beautiful wife is dark. These are our black women, no matter what her skin tone is. An attitude can be changed but her beauty is non-negotiable. Who cares about the outside when it's the inside that matters? All of these women are beautiful in their own way; they each bring something to the table and should be treated with love and respect. We can't be afraid of them brothers because they mean too much to us. They come in all shapes and sizes … find you a good one and romance her.

Especially you average Joe characters. You need to stop being afraid of these women because you feel you have nothing to offer. Don't allow her looks to intimidate you to the point where you won't speak to her. You have to make adjustments by making yourself appealing to her. Make sure your personal hygiene's are in order. Shave, get a haircut, and don't wear too much cologne or aftershave lotion. Check your breath, brush your teeth, and for God's sake use some body lotion or baby oil or Vaseline. Approach her with confidence and nothing less. If you're a big (heavy) man you don't have to be sloppy or tacky; not all muscle men have the ladies. Remember, first impressions are lasting impressions and you definitely want to impress her with your best. If she's got to make a choice, don't make it too easy for her.

However unfortunate, men are guided by what we see at first glance of the opposite sex. But it is important to remember that just like the cover of a book, one shouldn't judge by the outside. Brothers it is essential that you make your inner self-consistent with your outer self. Do what is necessary for you to represent the best you. Consistency, self-assurance, sincerity, and wit are pertinent ingredients for the black woman to make a sound choice. If romancing her is worth it and she is not use to this kind of man …get her use to it.

CHAPTER IX

LITTLE THINGS

I was talking with a group of professional women who said, "If men paid enough attention to the little things, the relationship would go a lot smoother." It's not the big things that really matter, although they count, it's the things that men tend to take for granted. Such as, helping around the house, getting the kids ready for school or bed, cooking dinner every once in a while, doing the laundry or even washing the dishes. For some reason most of you brothers have been taught that this is women's work ...not! These are just some of the things that will cause her not to feel neglected and that you genuinely take an interest in her. Another thing is giving her space. Most women hate to be crowded or feeling smothered by a man. She has to feel like she has her own individuality and her man should be able to recognize when she needs to be by herself.

Noticing the little things will decrease the stress level in a relationship because no one person is overloaded with all the work and you make time for each other. I remember conducting a survey about relationships a few years ago and the results were not surprising. The key items to a stressful relationship are the mismanagement of finances, the lack of communication, and the fear of intimacy (not willing to please your partner in provocative ways). While it is true we all have bills there's no need for them to stress us out. Black people need to learn how to manage their finances and stop budgeting from paycheck to paycheck. We get into more fights and arguments about money than we do about anything. If we learned how to communicate with one another instead of talking at each other (you bitch this …you bastard that …you ain't nothing but a dog …damn you) we could change the way some of our relationships are headed. Brothers, our black queens are not stress bearers; stop stressing them out! She's already handling more than she probably needs to and you adding stress cause more headaches for her.

My wife started a new job a year and a half ago. With it came a supervisory position and more responsibilities. With me continuing my education on a fulltime basis, two children in school, and the daily routine of running our household I knew I had to pick up the slack. Some days I cook dinner, some days I do the laundry but everyday I wash dishes. I pay the bills and we both do the grocery shopping. If there were no romance in our relationship then this ship would have sailed a long time ago all alone or sunk. We keep the romance alive by keeping the possibilities hopeful. We still go on dates like we did when we were courting, not as often but enough to keep the home fires burning. Most importantly, we've remained the best of friends throughout the course of our time together. This is key to romance in a relationship, friendship.

I was talking with a friend (who is involved with a man 15 years her senior for the last three months) about how he does so much for her. He's helped her move into her new home, he's cleaned her new place while she's working, he's washed her car regularly, and he's even trimmed her mother's bushes. She claims to be *romantically challenged* and she's not used to all this attention, this being her very first <u>real</u> romantic relationship. But in her mind he is a welcomed breath of fresh air because he's been saving her a lot of time when she works so many hours. Can you see what's so obvious? She spends a great deal of time at work and he spends a great deal of time doing for her when she's not there. Where's the romance? Many times because this is so new (romance) men and women often shy away from these new feelings because it seems to complicate their lives. When you're so used to being the "top dog" in your relationship you tend not to want to give up your individuality, when in fact you're not, you're just taking your life to another level. Don't be so afraid of the unknown, go with the flow, no one has to be romantically challenged. Although there is the appearance of commitment it seems that they're both afraid to verbalize it and so they're going through this major adjustment period. She is adjusting to something new in a relationship while he's adjusting to trusting a relationship because he's been hurt in the past. This is really normal and they'll eventually get through it or find out that it was never meant to be; but they will learn and grow from the experience.

Like a lot of black men, he has been hurt by a past relationship. So the question you may be asking yourself is, "Why is he trying so hard?" Or "Is he just a good hearted person with good intentions?" I posed this thought because some men tend to over-do things in a relationship to the point of almost smothering his black queen. Considering the fact that it's only been three months, it would seem to me that he has marriage on his mind —or to say that he sees a more permanent future for the two of them. This is what I call the "I can't lose her syndrome", or "I've found a good thing and I don't want to mess it up syndrome". Black men have a problem with giving too much so early into a relationship and ultimately wind up pushing her away unintentionally. This is why it is very important not to move so quickly in a relationship because you can become over zealous in your efforts to please and make a lot of unnecessary mistakes.

In another conversation with a male friend, I asked him, "Do you think men tried too hard in relationships only to make the same mistakes over again? Or do we really learn from our mistakes?" His answer was, "Men try to impress their black queen with material things instead of winning her heart with sincerity". Doing little things doesn't mean you have to overcompensate by doing everything that comes to mind. Sometimes you can do more harm than good if you're not careful. The following formula was created to see how many brothers are willing to admit to their selves where they are in life before actually committing to a relationship:

Wisdom = experience + maturity; $(W = e + m)$

Age + wisdom − maturity = young + dumb. $(A + W - m = Y + D)$

There are old ships and there are new ships but there is no ship like friendship. Romance makes the trip worthwhile.

Chapter X

Single Black Mothers

One would think that dating a single black mother is very difficult. How it is possible to fit romance in a relationship when her time is monopolized by her child? More to the point, is she looking for a "baby's daddy" in you and if there is a multiplicity of children how many "baby's daddy" do you have to compete with? Not meaning to offend the sisters, brothers these are legitimate questions you must ask yourself. Otherwise you may find yourself in a quandary of sorts; what to do when you don't know what to do? Proceed with caution. I want to share with you three different situations that may or may not influence your decision about dating the single black mother.

SBM #1: When I met this adult woman, she had two children, an older daughter and a young son. She was living at home with her mother while receiving government assistant. Each child had a different father, and then she got pregnant with her third child by another father who would later be killed leaving the child fatherless. After having this child she had a set of twins the next year and then another the following year, all totaling six children by four different fathers. When last I saw her, she was still receiving some assistance and living with the last children's father still in her mother's home. This is a woman who had everything going for her. She was quite spoken, intelligent, beautiful, and talented. So what happened?

SBM #2: She is an attractive woman with nine children by eight different fathers. She also receives government assistant but is now working because the child welfare system is cracking down on women having babies just for the money. She can't seem to keep a man because she's too busy giving them want they want, in the end finding herself with another mouth to feed. Do you see a self-esteem pattern?

SBM #3: She was married and had five children then divorced because her husband loved crack more than he loved his family. She took on the responsibility of raising her children alone, working two jobs and hiring a child care sitter. She then meets a single black father with two children of his own and they find the time to begin a relationship. A couple of years later they marry and he's feeling trapped because things aren't what they appear to be. What he thought was love turned out to be lust and he wasn't ready to be a stepfather ... to five kids. Both of them are very talented and believe in taking care of their family. They both work two jobs. They satisfied their physical needs for one another but didn't explore the path of romance too much. Will they make it?

The lesson from each of these similar situations is that single black mothers come as a package deal. Whether it's one or nine children. So when you are considering a romance, think about the entire package. Because romance becomes an adventure when you are romancing the entire package. You have to know which of these women you are willing to romance if any of them. You have to look at the big picture and decide whether or not you are ready for an instant family.

Consider your own children and how they would feel if you spent more time with someone else's children than you do with them. I remember a time when black fathers took the roll of being a family man very seriously. It didn't matter if these were his kids or not, he became **daddy**. He provided for the family, disciplined when it was considered necessary, and taught the life lessons for his children to survive. I grew up with my stepfather but always recognized him as "dad" because that's who he's always been to me. I'm now a stepfather to my youngest daughter and my wife is stepmother to our son, but the point is that we are family. We were willing to come together as a unit and raise our children together just as our parents raised us.

Brothers you can't knock the single black mother because most of you were raised by one of them. I agree some of them are not very responsible for having more children than they can handle. However, I do not suggest nor do I condone any man demeaning the single black mother. If anything brothers, we should be mature enough to encourage these women to do all they can to make a brighter future for their children. Some of these women are very productive and have raised some the most caring black men our society has to offer. Who knows, you could be one of them.

———⟫•◦•⟪———

CHAPTER XI

EXPECTATIONS

My wife and I were talking one day about the idea of meeting our expectations of each other. She was saying to me that we should have sat down before we were married, at the beginning of our romantic journey, and discussed what we expected from each other during this relationship. However, we were mature enough to discuss things as we have gone along. This is where many relationships fail because often times we don't recognize that we both come into this situation with some kind of expectancies but never take the opportunity to say anything because we're just happy "being in love." When you really think about it, a relationship is very much like operating a business. Every business begins with a business plan and a set of goals; likewise, every relationship should begin with a plan and goals. Every so often you must revisit those plans to see what goals have been met. The reason is because like a business, relationships tend to grow and change. Here's a story about a couple that went through a similar kind of thing and is surviving:

They met and for five wonderful weeks they shared a love affair, full of passion, excitement, and togetherness. Then tragedy struck, he became very ill with a life threatening condition, and had to be rushed to the hospital. Surgery had to be performed but before they took him away to the operating room, he said to her "I don't know if I'll come out of this or not, but I do know I love you." Even though they never saw this coming, they somehow managed to fall in love during that five-week period. After a long surgery he was taken to recovery where without hesitation she slept between two chairs until she knew he was going to be all right. They had built a bond but he never expected her to stay and she really didn't know what to expect. That was seven years ago and they're still together growing and changing, living and learning, loving and romancing.

When researching this topic I turned to the television and watched Divorce Court with Judge Mablean Ephraim who has the untiring task of dealing with couples who need to discuss the details of their divorce in a public forum. This is one of those shows that I think black people need to stay away from (no disrespect to Judge Ephraim) because all you're doing is showing how ignorant you are for five-minutes of fame. You're making your personal business a comedy for a television audience not only around the nation but also in your hometown …where people know (duh)! It's the couples that have been married for less than two years that I find somewhat brain-dead when it comes to understanding what this thing is all about. They all say the same thing "before we got married we did everything together, then after we got married he/she changed". That's because during their dating period they didn't discuss what expectations they had for a potential life mate.

This 28-year old black man and his 25-year-old wife were divorcing after one and a half years of marriage. He worked five days a week and all she had to do was take care of the children, keep the house clean, cook his lunch and dinner, and have his bath water ready when he came home from work. Her argument was that he was a chauvinist who never said any of these things when they were dating. It wasn't until after they were married that he decided to revert to what he felt couples did in the "50's and 60's". The judge had some mixed feelings about the situation until he said he wanted his bath water run with the water temperature just right. This is where he went from the sublime to the ridiculous with his expectations, because he couldn't acknowledge that what his wife was doing was also considered work. One woman was married to a man who she said loved her too much. He worked outside the home 70 hours per week, provided everything she needed and then some and it still weren't enough. She didn't want to have sex with him, she wasn't passionate or affectionate, and she couldn't understand why he loved her like this. His only explanation was that "she is my black queen". There are many instances of this type of nonsense on this show; I call these ridiculous expectations. Some black men have them and what's worse is some black women put up with this craziness. Some black women have them and some black men I am ashamed to say put up with the same bizarre craziness.

The only way to insure a productive future with your relationship is to talk about your expectations before this goes any further. You have to know what you are getting yourself into before you leap. Listed below is a recap of things you should follow when romancing the black woman:

- Be a man, respect and love yourself, take care of your business and your responsibilities in a mature way.
- Treat the black woman as a black queen with royalty.
- Be honest and truthful.
- Be creative especially financially.

43

- Be secure, well-adjusted, and never let jealousy intervene in your relationship.

- Have a sense of humor and strong self esteem. Never allow a strong black woman to intimidate you.

- Have a strong faith based foundation. You can't go wrong with the Word of God unless you go too far. Let the Spirit lead you to a place of peace.

- Be sensitive to the black woman, be understanding to her plight as the backbone of our society. Give her the respect that she so richly deserves.

- Be sincere, take your time, and remember the little things.

- A black woman's attitude can change but her beauty is non-negotiable.

- There is no real definitive description of romance because it is a learned behavior.

- Use common sense.

⟫◦⟪

CHAPTER XII

FRIENDS

On New Years Eve 1996, I was on air at the radio station and during one of my breaks I received a phone from a former friend whom I had known for a few years. While she and I were talking, I jokingly asked her if she had any single friends. She replied in the affirmative and I put her on hold as I was still working. When I returned to the conversation, to my surprise, she had called her single friend and introduced us. "D. Kelly this is Nina and Nina this is D. Kelly" I thought to myself "I was just joking." Now, prior to this introduction I remember my friend saying that her single friend was just like her and I thought "God I hope not!" Anyway, Nina and I spoke briefly and I found out that her birthday was a couple of days away so I decided to take this opportunity to meet her. Let me just say that if there are any radio jocks reading this please be warned, **not all pretty voices look the part.** One has to be very careful of the infamous blind date. She might sound good and may say she looks good but the proof is in the pudding. Fortunately for me this was not the case.

I had a plan to meet this mysterious woman I had the pleasure of speaking with on the phone. But my goal was to meet her during the day in case she didn't look the part. She opened her door and to my surprise stood the most beautiful creature I'd seen in quite sometime. Her eyes sparkled (literally) her smile was incredibly bright and as a matter of confirmation that she was the one …we were wearing the same colors. I made up my mind upon first sight that she would be my wife. Two years eight months later my childhood friend Ken Price married us after a Sunday morning church service at the Corinthian Baptist Church. I've never looked back and regretted one day.

This past New Year's Eve Nina received a phone call after eight years from that same friend who wanted to congratulate us on being together for as long as we have been. I'm sure she never would have guessed that we'd last this long but we have a lifetime contract …until death do us part. The fact is that she was the instrument used to bring us together, that was the blessing; the curse was she had her doubts. Although she never voiced them to me her actions and her sudden withdrawal of friendship led me to believe otherwise. The lesson learned here, is your happiness with the person you finally choose, as a mate is not contingent upon anyone else's happiness. If you like them, then I love them!

It is so very important for each individual to understand that no one has the right to decide for you whom you have a romantic interest in except God. He created man for woman and woman for man and it's not up to us to go against the righteous order of our Creator. Neither is it any friends' place, no matter how much she thinks you're alike, to offer an opinion unless asked. In this respect friends can either be a blessing or a curse, you need to decide for yourself. The Bible says, "He that has friends must first show himself friendly". I know for some of us friendship is hard to come by but for others we have tons of friends …just don't let them get into your romantic business because it's personal.

Now it's not so strange to think that some of our friends who call themselves being in love are a little naïve. Sometimes they can't seem to recognize the traits of repetition in their relationships as they often times seem to end up with the same type of person. Sometimes it takes a ***real friend*** who is not selfish or self-centered, to help you realize what you're doing to yourself. We learn early on who our real friends are, whom we can count on, who we can or cannot trust and whom we can depend on for their honesty without being condescending or critical.

A few years ago I was reading a magazine article that asked the questioned, "Can men and women be friends without intimacy?" to this I say yes. But sometimes women use this "we can be friends" line to feel safe or because she's really not that into you. There's nothing wrong, brothers, with being friends with a beautiful woman. As a matter of fact there are advantages to having a woman as a friend. Because if you're involved in a relationship that you're unsure about the signals she is sending you then you can get clarity from your female friend …also there's someone to tell you truthfully about you. Now when it comes to male/female friendships wisdom must be applied. If your friend has a tendency to be somewhat jealous of you relationship(s) with another female then you may want to examine their feelings for you. Don't get caught saying, "I didn't know" or "I thought we were just friends" **PAY ATTENTION TO THE SIGNS MAN**! She'll be dropping hints like raindrops on a sunny day.

This happened to a real good friend of mine. He wasn't paying attention to his close friend who was falling for him while he was getting involved with the woman who would later become his wife. Now, one can't control who the heart falls in love with but the heart must be sensitive to others you surround yourself with. He honestly did not share the same feelings his friend had for him because he was pre-occupied with his busy lifestyle and this new woman in his life. So after the wedding, the friend just disappeared into the abyss of nowhere. No one has heard from her since although I believe she is doing okay now.

After being in a marriage for nearly two decades a man and his wife were divorced. Through this marriage he was diligent, dedicated, and devoted to his wife and family. There were some very rough moments during their time together and he took the divorce pretty hard. Needless to say, he survived and began dating one year after his divorce became final. In that year he had time to reflect and think about the kind of woman he wanted to share the rest of his life with. Instead of depending on his own ideals he turned to his faith where he felt secure believing God would give him his choice mate. In the meantime, he met a couple friends that seemed to be interested in him, both completely opposite of one another. However, the problem was that they were colleagues in his work place (usually not a good idea), but they were friends. Until one, (we'll call her the church lady), became possessively aggressive and insanely jealous because she felt that he didn't have a right to talk to other women while he was talking to her. The other female, (we'll call her butter), was rather laid back and really wasn't interested in a serious relationship because her past relationships weren't that successful. Because he wasn't obligated to either of the ladies, he had no accountability to them. However, "the church lady" was always on the defensive and this continued to push him away whereas "butter" was more interested in his general well being and not causing him any drama. One relationship reminded him of what he didn't want in, while the other relationship was on course to what could lead to a place of sheer happiness.

The moral of this is, friendship is an awesome gift to have and just like a brain …a terrible thing to waste. Choose your friends carefully as they may or may not play a role in your romantic journey. Remember friends are sensitive too.

———⬗◉⬔———

CHAPTER XIII

RECIPROCATE

This book is not based on scientific fact but rather actual experiences. I wrote this book initially out of frustration because I couldn't understand why our society places so much value on the romantic lifestyle of other races and not so much on ours. Then I began to see a pattern from black filmmakers over the last 10 years. However amusing some of these movies may be, there's still some representation of romance amid black people. My second reason for writing this book was because I felt a sense of obligation to encourage black men from every walk of life to begin to romance black women and change our societal status. My third reason was because I have two daughters and it's important to me that when they choose a mate, that they leave no stones unturned. I want them to make sure they understand what kind of man would be best suited for them as a life partner. As well as for my son who will follow in my footsteps but hopefully not make the same mistakes I made.

I also wrote this for the Black Queen, who hasn't been romanced. You deserve to be romanced and you should not accept anything less than that. In this book I have shared some valuable information with the black man, which the black woman can also use. You need to make the first step by taking your time. Along the way you will encounter jealousy and other negativity but you can't let them influence you in anyway. Don't act so spoiled when a man is attempting to be financially creative. It is not necessary that you tear down his ego. I'm sure you've had to be just as financially creative when you didn't have enough money. Take a hard look at your self-esteem, your level of self-confidence and raise the bar. Don't take what I say as gospel but as a way of measuring the kind of men, women may desire in their lives. There is no real definitive description of romance because it is a learned behavior. We absorb what we see from our parents, grandparents, neighbors, where we go to church, or the club. It's the portrayal that we perceive from music videos, the movies, and even romantic novels. We take a little bit from each and try to emulate or incorporate these different styles into our own romantic activities.

The steps to romancing the black woman start with understanding what romance is and where it begins. The next step is how black women need for black men to be sincere. Next, understanding that you must make time to get to know her, be honest and creative allowing her to see the real you. Try to communicate as much as possible and keep all negative influences out of your romantic journey. Verbal communication will eliminate all of the presumptions, assumptions, and can't talk moments. Practice being positive and don't allow the color of her skin to be a factor. **ALL BLACK WOMEN ARE BEAUTIFUL**. Remember integrity, morality, and spirituality are the foundation of your relationship and will carry you through some of the roughest times. Friendship is the glue that holds these attributes together.

You may find this book to be somewhat sophomoric in content but rest assure what's missing from a great people is a little known item called *common sense*. Seems we've forgotten how to use it with all the technological thinking our society has to offer. Has your overall question been answered? What is romance? You probably feel there are more don'ts in this book than there are do's but we learn from our mistakes and hopefully we gain experience and wisdom. All the information in this book shared with the black man is also meant for the black woman. Get to know him first before you make any irrational decisions and don't rush to get him to the altar. When in doubt use **common sense.** You are not alone in your decision making process about romance. Men deal with some of the same issues you deal with everyday. It is important ladies that you understand everything you desire from a man, in some way deep down inside, he desires from you …you have to help him find it.

When all else fails P.U.S.H, pray until something happens.

POETRY

From the book entitled "Lyrical Romance"

The following poetry is from the soon to be released "Lyrical Romance" from the award winning International Library of Poetry member, Dale J Kelly.

MY LOVE FOR YOU

Wait a minute don't go! I love you! I love you.
It's not too late for us …is it?
What will it take for you to love me?
What about the good times?
What about the times we've …shared?
How can you tear my heart from me, how can you shred the very core of my love for you?
I can't breathe without you.
I can't think without you, can't live without …you.

Do you have any ideal how much you mean to me?
Do you even know the depth, the height, or the width of my love?

Can your imagination even comprehend the unlimited
boundaries that my love universally surrounds your entire
being with?
I love you more than life itself.
Without you there's no me.

The snow-capped mountains of Mt. Everest are not high enough.
The bottom of the deepest ocean is not deep enough.
The entire galaxy with the consolation of stars, the planets,
and the Milky Way is not wide enough to keep my love from
reaching …only you.
You see …I love you.
I love you with a love that no man can love you with and is
second only to the Creator because He is the originator of
the love I have for you.

DJK

A Love Hiku

Black like beauty is
A skin-deep proposition
To eyes beholden

DJK

A Life With You

A life with you is to me a life of blissful eternity
A life with you is to me more than any words could speak
A life with you is to me where happiness resides in me
Although it was hard to find you brought it out of its gentle
sleep

A life with you is more to me than a simple melody
Not just a song a rhythm or a rhyme
It's a life without skipping a beat in time
It's the orchestrated concert of lyrical romance
The ballet of quarter notes in an unrehearsed dance
It's an uncharted sheet of music that when played
Sings a melodious song of forever plus one day

A life with you is to me a life of spirituality
When our broken souls became as one
It birthed a union and life begun,
A life with you...

DJK

A Poem For Nina

Your eyes glimmered like a crystal vase
As I gazed upon your lovely dark face
Skin so supple and smooth to the touch
Made me want and desire you so very much

You looked at me with love in your eyes
It was then I knew you would be my wife
And so this day I pledge my undying love to you
Weathering together, we'll make it through

Until that day when death do we part
You will always forever have claim on my heart

DJK

Declaration Of Love

Love o love of mine
Is the sweet song my heart sings
When words cannot be uttered from my lips
I pray you feel as I do
For romance this night will never be the same
As I declare my love for you

DJK

In Twenty Four Hours

The darkest hour is between night and day
The most glorious hour is the sun's early rise
The most beautiful hour is the setting sun
As each moment of time passes
Every hour, every minute, every second
Is made more lovely because
The most precious hour is spent with you

DJK

The Key

I
fy
ouc
anre
adthe
se
cret
inm
yhea
rtth
enyo
uha
veun
loc
kedt
hekey
tom
ylov
e,
you.

DJK

PRELUDE TO A ROMANCE

From the theatrical production "Pen Pals"

The following are excerpts from the play "Pen Pals" written and directed by Dale J. Kelly, produced by Second Chance Productions. It's the story of two African-American adults in their late 40's meeting through a singles column. The only stipulation to answering this advertisement is that he requests that she reply by handwritten letters. This is his way of weeding out the foolish from the serious.

WINTER

Dear Sir,

I don't know who you are or who you think you are but you have certainly aroused my curiosity. What makes a man desire a pen pal unless he's imprisoned or living in a castle somewhere as a deformed beast? Are you looking for your one and only beauty? Or are you looking to have someone waiting for you when you get out of prison? If this is the case you need not write me back.

It just baffles me how some men will do anything to attract a woman whom they think is vulnerable or a "dumb blond". In either case, I'm neither ...just a little curious to know what kind of man you are.

Signed,

Curiously Concerned

Dear C.C.

It is not my intention to mislead anyone to think I am some Shrek-like olger or death row inmate. I apologize if I made you feel this way. I take this very seriously because you never know who's going to write you back. Some female who's been locked up for killing her last man or some ugly duckling hoping to meet her Prince Charming that he may ride in on his white horse and save her from the wicked stepmother? I have to be just as careful as you seem to be.

My goal was to meet someone who had an adventurous side to them and would take the time needed to get to know someone as a friend through the mail; basically, a pen pal. Now the question is, are you the one to meet this challenge?

Signed,

Perfectly Sane

The winter months have nearly ended and spring is approaching as these two have continued writing, developing a strong foundation of friendship. After sometime of writing back and forth the two are finally on a first name basis, but still replying to separate post office boxes for anonymity.

SPRING

Dear Quincy,

I received you letter today and I was so happy to hear from you. It seems to me that we are probably the only two people left in the world who actually find the time to write letters to one another. It's funny, I have this Dell computer sitting here and I hardly use it, but I guess its okay when this is so much more interesting. I received a call from my folks back home yesterday. Mom is doing well; Dad is missing me a whole lot because he never thought I'd leave our little city. He wants to kill my ex-husband for what he did and how he hurt me but I told him that God doesn't like ugly and he would get his in spades.

I am so looking forward to the beginning of spring; it's my favorite time of year. It's as though God has this way of telling us that the old has to die in order for the new to grow ...imagine that. I've wanted to take a tour of this big city of yours but the weather hasn't permitted it. Maybe, after an April shower when the rain smells the freshest you'll be my tour guide and I can see all the sights through your eyes. Wouldn't that be fun?

I can't wait to hear from you again.

Your friend,

Lenora

SUMMER

Dear Lenora,

Can you believe it's been nearly six months since we've been writing one another? So much has changed in my life since meeting you …I mean, from writing you. I feel as though I've known you my whole life and yet I've never even seen your face. I am longing to hear your voice for the first time; just to hear you say, hello. Wouldn't it be nice if more people could do what we're doing …getting to really know each other in a way that allows your imagination to be spontaneous?

Summer will be over soon and my favorite season is fast approaching. Autumn. I just get a kick out of how each season is as multi-colorful as the one before it but none like autumn. It's more subdued, more laid-back; it's like the perfect time for the perfect romance with the perfect woman. I'm anticipating that woman is …you. Not a day goes by when you're not on my mind. You've already captured my heart and to be quite honest with you, I think I'm falling in love with you.

Quincy

Dear Quincy,

When you told me two months ago that you were in love with me, my life became somewhat complete. I thought I had been for the last twenty years but I guess in hindsight I knew I wasn't. You have brought so much joy into my heart and we have become more than just friends, who would have thought? The only thing that will make me happier than I am right now is to be in your arms.

You are without question my best friend. You've made it so easy for me to be myself with you and I feel so content.

One would think if they were reading our letters that we were two crazy people …I mean, we don't know what each other look like. We've never physically met or ever spoken to one another. But I know in my heart that I will love you …until forever.

Love Always,

Lenora

FALL

Dear Lenora,

I look back and remember when we first started writing one another; you thought I was crazy. Little did I know then, that now I would be crazy about …you? It's been nearly an entire year and I think it's time that we put faces to these letters, wouldn't you agree? I have to be honest with you, I am a somewhat apprehensive toward the idea because I don't want you to be disappointed with me. I can't imagine living my life without you and now that I have found you, I don't ever want to loose you.

Everyday during this fall I have been walking through the park hoping to bump into you. However, that didn't happen but I did bump into this very nice lady who had the most beautiful eyes; and I prayed she were you. Only she was just a neighbor. We need to set up a time and date to make this official. (Thinking and looking at his calendar) What about Christmas? This will surely be an unforgettable holiday! What do you think?

Quincy

WINTER

Dear Quincy,

I would love for us to spend Christmas together but I have already made plans to go back home and spend that time with my parents. Is it possible to make our date on New Year's Eve, that way we can begin the New Year together. I promise you won't be disappointed; plus like you said, it will be an unforgettable holiday.

Incidentally, I had the same kind of bump in the park incident you had. I was coming home admiring the multiple colors, and I guess I wasn't paying much attention to where I was walking when I bumped into this very handsome stranger. He looked at me as though he were starring right through me, as though he knew me. I found out later that he was just a neighbor so it stands to reason why he looked as though he knew me. By chance, that wasn't you …was it?

I heard from my ex the other day and he totally surprised me. After almost a year I never thought I would hear from him again. He went on to tell me how much he missed me and that he was not with anyone at the present time. He also said that he had cleaned up his act and was now ready to be with the only woman he's ever loved …me. Then he asked me to come back to him and I stop him and said, "You didn't want me when you had me so what makes you think I would come back to something like you. Hell, I'm still wearing your name; what more do you want? Besides I'm perfectly happy with the new love I have in my life and he's more man than you'll ever be …thanks for the memories!" And with that said I exhaled.

Quincy, you would have been proud of me. But more importantly that baggage is in the trash and I'm free to be with you.

Forever yours

Dear Lenora,

Life has a way of finding the right time, the right elements, and the right people it wants to place in our lives. In one week all these things will come together as you and I will spend our first embrace on New Years Eve. I can hardly wait. I have longed for this day for an entire year and nothing will keep me from it. Here are the directions to the restaurant we'll be meeting at. On the table will be a single white orchid in a crystal vase, I will be in a black tuxedo with and angel pendant attached to my right lapel. I will be facing the door so that I don't miss your entrance.

Until then my darling, I love you.

Simultaneously both Lenora and Quincy come out of their apartments with their backs to one another then as on cue, turn and face each other. Lenora immediately notices the angel pendant and with hesitation in her voice she speaks:

Lenora

(Surprised by the pendant) That's a lovely pendant you're wearing. (Almost afraid to go on with the conversation)

Quincy

(With a big smile on his face) Thank you. I'm wearing it for a very special lady tonight. This and a single white ... (Lenora interrupts him by finishing his sentence)

Lenora

...White orchid in a crystal vase. (They pause as though they're both stunned. Then simultaneously they exclaim) YOU!

Quincy

YOU!! All this time and you were right across the hall from me.

Lenora

Me. What about you? No wonder you stared at me so hard in the park.

Laughter breaks out between them and finally an embrace and their first kiss.

Lenora

So what do we do now?

Quincy

Let's go to dinner and discuss it. At least we don't have to take two cars.

Lenora

Then what? (She looks at Quincy and he shrugs his shoulders) Well, I guess we'll cross that threshold when we get back. (Fade to black)

THE END

ENDNOTES

1. Johnson, Bud "Man of The House" is becoming a misnomer <u>African-American News & Issues</u> 6 Nov. 2003 Father's Day 2003

2. AmeriStat, tabulations from the Census Bureau's <u>Current Population Survey</u> (March Supplement), various years

3. Johnson, Bud "Man of The House" is becoming a misnomer <u>African-American News & Issues</u> 6 Nov. 2003 Father's Day 2003

4. James Brown, It's A Man's World

5. Genesis 2:18, 21-23

6. Ephesians 5:21-24

7. Hebrews 11:1, Now, faith is the substance of things hoped for, the evidence of things not seen.

8. Proverbs 2:16, 5:3, 5:20, 6:24, 7:5

9. Exodus 20:17

10. Ephesians 5:20